AL•LEONARD
ro vocal®
BETTER THAN KARAOKE!

Walt Disney
PICTURES PRESENTS

ENCHANTED

WOMEN/MEN EDITION
VOLUME 2

Disney characters and artwork © Disney Enterprises, Inc.

ISBN 978-1-4234-6045-9

HAL•LEONARD®
CORPORATION
7777 W. BLUEMOUND RD. P.O. BOX 13819 MILWAUKEE, WI 53213

WALT DISNEY MUSIC COMPANY
WONDERLAND MUSIC COMPANY, INC.

In Australia Contact:
Hal Leonard Australia Pty. Ltd.
4 Lentara Court
Cheltenham, Victoria, 3192 Australia
Email: ausadmin@halleonard.com.au

Visit Hal Leonard Online at
www.halleonard.com

CONTENTS

Ever Ever After

Music by Alan Menken
Lyrics by Stephen Schwartz

Happy Working Song

Music by Alan Menken
Lyrics by Stephen Schwartz

song. _____

Bridge

Oh, how strange a place to
be 'til Ed-ward comes for me, my heart is sigh - ing.
Still, as long as I am here, I guess a new ex - per - i - ence could
be worth try - ing. Hey, keep dry - ing!

Chorus

You could do a lot when you've got such a hap-py work-ing tune to hum
while you're spong-ing up the soap - y scum. We a - dore each
filth - y chore that we de - ter - mine. So, friends, e - ven though you're

ver - min, we're a hap - py work - ing

song. _____ Sing - ing as we fetch the de -

ter - gent box or the smel - ly shirts and the stink - y socks.

Sing a - long. If you can - not sing, then hum a - long

as we're fin - ish - ing our hap - py work - ing

Outro

song. _____ Ah,

was - n't this fun? ___

So Close

Music by Alan Menken
Lyrics by Stephen Schwartz

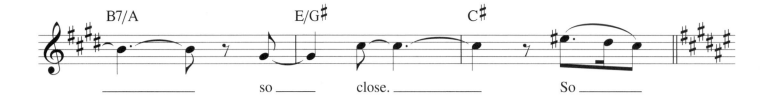

so _____ close. _____ So _____

Chorus

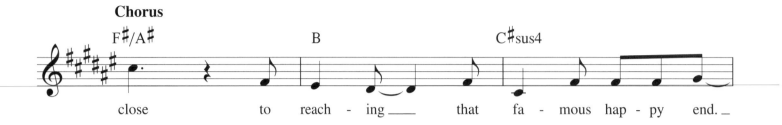

close to reach - ing _____ that fa - mous hap - py end. _____

_____ Al - most be - liev - ing _____

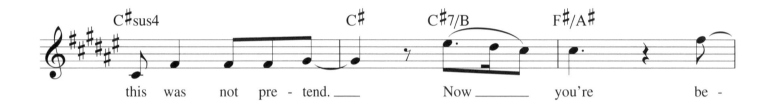

this was not pre - tend. _____ Now _____ you're be -

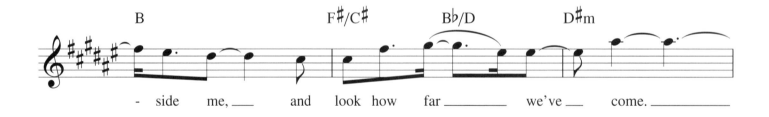

- side me, _____ and look how far _____ we've _____ come. _____

_____ So _____ far _____ we _____

Interlude

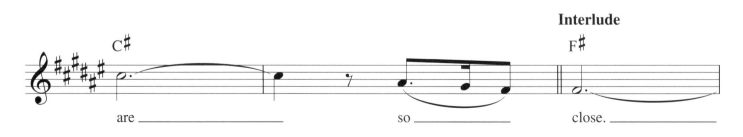

are _____ so _____ close. _____

Chorus

so _____ close to reach - ing _____ that

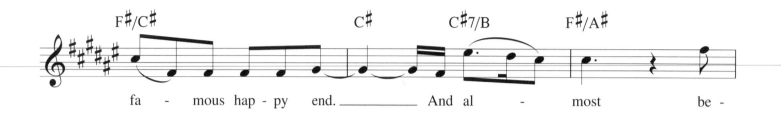

fa - mous hap - py end. _____ And al - most be -

liev - ing _____ this was not pre - tend. _____ Let's go _____

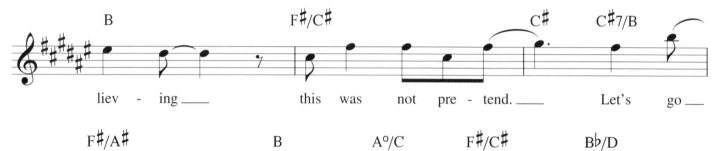

_____ on dream - ing, _____ for we know _____ we

Rubato

are. _____ So

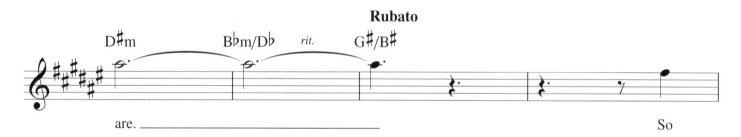

close, _____ so close _____ and still _____ so

Outro

far. _____

far. _____

That's Amoré
(That's Love)

Words by Jack Brooks
Music by Harry Warren

Intro
Moderately Slow

Moderately Fast

Bells will ring, ting - a - ling - a - ling, ting - a - ling - a -

ling, and you'll sing, "Vi - ta Bel - la." _____

Hearts will play tip - py, tip - py

tay, tip - py, tip - py tay, like a gay tar - an -

tel - la. _____ When the

Verse

stars _____ make you drool _____ just like pas - ta fa -

zool, that's _ a - mor - é. _____

When you dance down the street with a

that's ___ a - mor - é. _____

That's a -

mor - é.

5

B♭

That's a - mor - é. _____

2

B♭/D

B♭o/D♭   F7/C   F7   **6**   B♭

Luck - y fel - la.

When

Verse

the   stars   make   you   drool   just   like

B♭/D B♭o/D♭   F7/C   F7

pas - ta fa - zool,   that's ___ a - mor - é. _____

3

When   you   dance _____ down   the

street with a cloud at your feet, _____ you're in

love. _____ When you

Rubato

walk in a dream but you know you're not

a tempo

dream - ing, si - gno - re.

Scuz - za me, but you see back in

Outro

old Nap - o - li, that's a - mor - é. _____

That's a - mor - é. _____

That's How You Know

Music by Alan Menken
Lyrics by Stephen Schwartz

that you love her? How do you show her you love her?

How does she know that you real - ly, real - ly, tru -

Verse

D   Gsus2/D   Asus4/D

- ly love her? It's not e - nough to take ___ the one you love for

D   Gsus2/D   Asus/D   D   Gsus2/D

grant - ed. _____   You must re - mind her, or ___

Asus/D   B   G♯m   Asus   A

___ she'll be in - clined to say,   "How do I know ___

Chorus

D   Gsus2   Asus   D   Gsus2

_____   he _____ loves me? ___

Asus   D   Gsus2   Asus   B   G♯m

How do I know _____   he's   mine?" _____

E/B   F♯   B   E

___ Well, does he   leave a lit - tle note to tell ___ you you ___ are

on his ___ mind? ___ Send _ you yel - low flow - ers

when the sky is gray? Hey. _____

He'll find a new way to show you ___ a lit - tle bit ev - 'ry

day. That's how __ you know,

Interlude

that's how _ you know he's ____ your _____ love. _____

Vocals 1st time only

Verse

Ev - 'ry - bod - y wants to live _

___ hap - pi - ly ev - er af - ter. _____

Chorus

25

True Love's Kiss

Music by Alan Menken
Lyrics by Stephen Schwartz

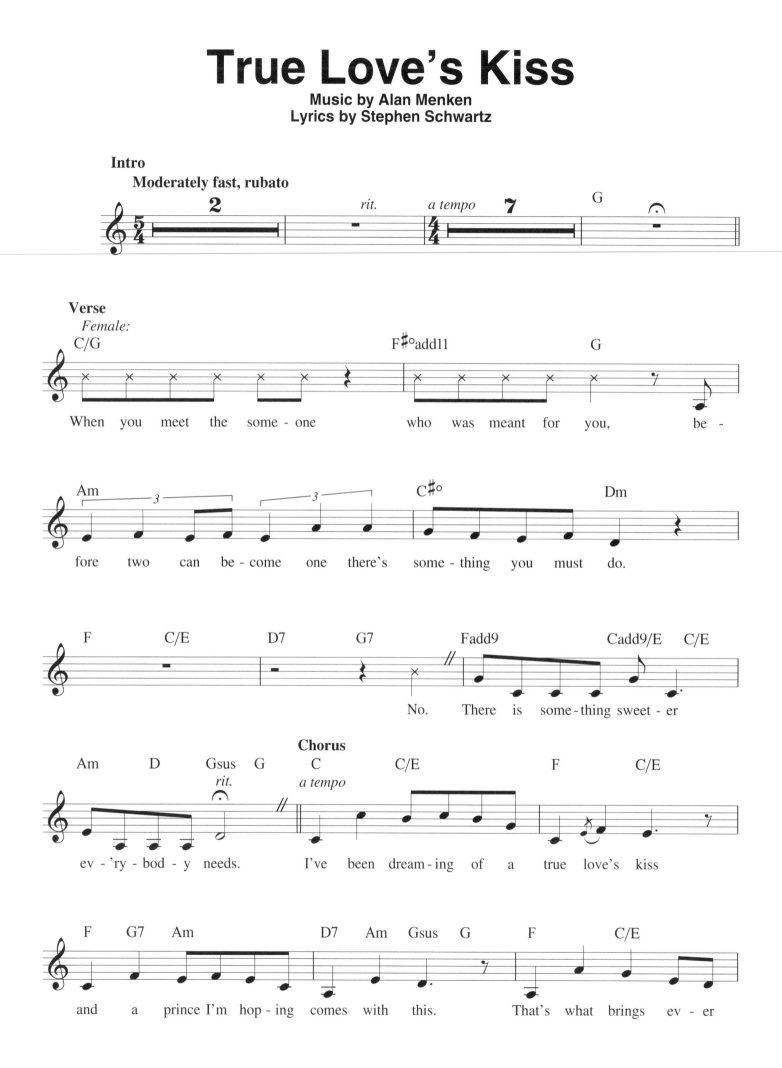

Chorus

Pro Vocal® Series
SONGBOOK & SOUND-ALIKE CD
SING 8 CHART-TOPPING SONGS WITH A PROFESSIONAL BAND

Whether you're a karaoke singer or an auditioning professional, the Pro Vocal® series is for you! Unlike most karaoke packs, each book in the ProVocal Series contains the lyrics, melody, and chord symbols for eight hit songs. The CD contains demos for listening, and separate backing tracks so you can sing along. The CD is playable on any CD player, but it is also enhanced so PC and Mac computer users can adjust the recording to any pitch without changing the tempo! Perfect for home rehearsal, parties, auditions, corporate events, and gigs without a backup band.

BROADWAY SONGS
00740247 Women's Edition......................................$12.95
00740248 Men's Edition...$12.95

MICHAEL BUBLÉ
00740362 Men's Edition...$14.95

CHRISTMAS HITS
00740396 Women's Edition......................................$14.95
00740397 Men's Edition...$14.95

CHRISTMAS STANDARDS
00740299 Women's Edition......................................$12.95
00740298 Men's Edition...$12.95

KELLY CLARKSON
00740377 Women's Edition......................................$14.95

PATSY CLINE
00740374 Women's Edition......................................$14.95

CONTEMPORARY CHRISTIAN
00740390 Women's Edition......................................$14.95
00740391 Men's Edition...$14.95

CONTEMPORARY HITS
00740246 Women's Edition......................................$12.95
00740251 Men's Edition...$12.95

MILEY CYRUS
00740394 Women's Edition......................................$14.95

DISCO FEVER
00740281 Women's Edition......................................$12.95
00740282 Men's Edition...$12.95

DISNEY'S BEST
00740344 Women's Edition......................................$14.95
00740345 Men's Edition...$14.95

DISNEY FAVORITES
00740342 Women's Edition......................................$14.95
00740343 Men's Edition...$14.95

'80S GOLD
00740277 Women's Edition......................................$12.95
00740278 Men's Edition...$12.95

ELLA FITZGERALD
00740378 Women's Edition......................................$14.95

GREASE
00740369 Women's Edition......................................$14.95
00740370 Men's Edition...$14.95

JOSH GROBAN
00740371 Men's Edition...$17.95

HAIRSPRAY
00740379 Women's Edition......................................$14.95

HANNAH MONTANA
00740375 Girl's Edition...$14.95

MORE HANNAH MONTANA
00740393 Girl's Edition...$14.95

HIGH SCHOOL MUSICAL 1 & 2
00740360 Women's Edition......................................$14.95
00740361 Guy's Edition..$14.95

HIP-HOP HITS
00740368 Men's Edition...$14.95

HITS OF THE '50S
00740381 Men's Edition...$14.95

HITS OF THE '60S
00740382 Men's Edition...$14.95

HITS OF THE '70S
00740384 Women's Edition......................................$14.95
00740383 Men's Edition $14.95

BILLIE HOLIDAY
00740388 Women's Edition......................................$14.95

JAZZ BALLADS
00740353 Women's Edition......................................$12.95

JAZZ FAVORITES
00740354 Women's Edition......................................$12.95

Prices, contents, & availability subject to change without notice.
Disney charaters and artwork © Disney Enterprises, Inc.

JAZZ STANDARDS
00740249 Women's Edition......................................$12.95
00740250 Men's Edition...$12.95

JAZZ VOCAL STANDARDS
0074037 Women's Edition..$14.95

BILLY JOEL
00740373 Men's Edition...$17.95

MOVIE SONGS
00740365 Women's Edition......................................$14.95
00740366 Men's Edition...$14.95

MUSICALS OF BOUBLIL & SCHÖNBERG
00740350 Women's Edition......................................$14.95
00740351 Men's Edition...$14.95

ELVIS PRESLEY
00740333 Volume 1...$14.95
00740335 Volume 2...$14.95

R&B SUPER HITS
00740279 Women's Edition......................................$12.95
00740280 Men's Edition...$12.95

FRANK SINATRA CLASSICS
00740347 Men's Edition...$14.95

FRANK SINATRA STANDARDS
00740346 Men's Edition...$14.95

THE SOUND OF MUSIC
00740389 Women's Edition......................................$14.95

TORCH SONGS
00740363 Women's Edition......................................$12.95
00740364 Men's Edition...$12.95

TOP HITS
00740380 Women's Edition......................................$14.95

VOCAL WARM-UPS
00740395 ....$14.95

ANDREW LLOYD WEBBER
00740348 Women's Edition......................................$14.95
00740349 Men's Edition...$14.95

WEDDING GEMS
00740309 Book/CD Pack Women's Edition $12.95
00740310 Book/CD Pack Men's Edition $12.95
00740311 Duets Edition..$12.95

WICKED
00740392 Women's Edition......................................$14.95

HANK WILLIAMS
00740386 Men's Edition...$14.95

0608

Visit Hal Leonard online at www.halleonard.com